Handbagged

Moira Buffini's plays include *Blavatsky's Tower* (Machine Room), *Gabriel* (Soho Theatre), *Silence* (Birmingham Rep), *Loveplay* (Royal Shakespeare Company), *Dinner* (National Theatre and West End), *Dying for It*, adapted from *The Suicide* by Nikolai Erdman (Almeida), *Vampire Story* (NT Connections), *Marianne Dreams* (Almeida) and *Welcome to Thebes* (National Theatre).

MOIRA BUFFINI
Handbagged

ff

faber and faber

First published in 2013
by Faber and Faber Limited
74–77 Great Russell Street
London WC1B 3DA

Revised reprint 2016

Typeset by Country Setting, Kingsdown, Kent CT14 8ES
Printed in England by CPI Bookmarque, Croydon, Surrey

A CIP record for this book is available from the British Library

ISBN 978-0-571-31250-4

4 6 8 10 9 7 5 3

For Susan Buffini

This play would not have been written
without the help and encouragement
of Indhu Rubasingham

Handbagged is a fictional account which has been inspired by true events. Incidents, characters and timelines have been changed for dramatic purposes. Often, the words are those imagined by the author. The play should not be understood as biography or any other kind of factual account.

Handbagged was first performed at the Tricycle Theatre, London, on 26 September 2013. The cast, in alphabetical order, was as follows:

Q Marion Bailey
T Stella Gonet
Liz Clare Holman
Actor 1 Neet Mohan
Actor 2 Jeff Rawle
Mags Fenella Woolgar

Director Indhu Rubasingham
Designer Richard Kent
Lighting Designer Oliver Fenwick
Sound Designer Carolyn Downing

Characters

T
an older Margaret Thatcher

Q
an older Queen Elizabeth II

Mags
a younger Margaret Thatcher

Liz
a younger Queen Elizabeth II

Actor 1
playing
A Palace Footman
Kenneth Kaunda
Nancy Reagan
Enoch Powell
Michael Shea
Neil Kinnock
Kenneth Clarke
A Protestor

Actor 2
playing
Denis Thatcher
Peter Carrington
Gerry Adams
Ronald Reagan
Michael Heseltine
Arthur Scargill
Rupert Murdoch
Geoffrey Howe
Prince Philip

HANDBAGGED

Mrs Thatcher, elderly. She prepares to address us.

T   Freedom
Freedom and democracy
They are things worth dying for.
We must never
Never stop resisting those who would take them
from us
And when they have been taken
We will fight until we get them back.

The act of resistance is our defining act as
human beings.
To say 'No, I will not stand for that,'
I will not collude, collaborate, negotiate
I will not compromise'
To say to the enemies of freedom 'You are
wrong'
To resist, whatever the cost

To say No

This is courage
This is integrity.
I would be proud if this word defined me:

NO

I'd like a chair
I don't need one but I'd like one
I will not ask for one
If I wait, they will notice

They will bring me one

One of the men

Dancing around me in their suits
Ties flapping in the wind.
Holding their documents like babies
The men
I could pin them wriggling with my gaze
And then release them with a smile
I liked to do it
Girlish
I was girlish

*Queen Elizabeth II enters dragging a chair. She
is elderly.*

Q   You look as if you need a chair

T   I'm quite capable of standing, thank you

Q   I'm bringing you a chair

T   There really isn't any need

     The Queen places it.

Q   Here

T   No thank you

Q   I've gone and brought it now, sit down

T   Thank you, no

     Pause.

Q   We conceive parliamentary institutions, with
     their free speech and respect for the rights of
     minorities, to be a precious part of our way of
     life and outlook. They inspire a broad tolerance
     in thought and expression.
     During recent centuries, this message has been

4

sustained and invigorated by the immense
contribution, in language, literature, and action,
of the nations of our Commonwealth overseas.
Our Commonwealth gives expression, as I pray
it always will, to living principles as sacred to
the Crown and Monarchy as to its many
Parliaments and Peoples. I ask you now to
cherish them - and practise them too; then we
can go forward together in peace, seeking justice
and freedom for all men

T   Why don't you sit down?

Q   No thank you

        Pause.

        What can one say here?

Q   How far can one go?

T   Oh, don't hold back
        It's all beyond our control

Q   Indeed

T   All artifice and sham

Q   I've never been fond of the theatre

T   No

Q   We saw *War Horse* recently
        We liked the horses

T   One would like to speak frankly

Q   One doesn't want to blab

T   Oh no, there's nothing worse than a blabber
        We have never blabbed

Q   Whatever we say must stay between these three
        walls

T	Nothing uncontrolled No outpouring
Q	Then we'd better have some tea. When one needs to control the pouring Tea can be most reassuring

TWO: MAY THE FOURTH BE WITH YOU

*A younger Queen (Liz) and a younger Thatcher
(Mags) enter.*

Mags	We knew we had won by the early hours of May the fourth. Finchley roared with jubilation Maggie Maggie Hours later it was still thundering in my ears
Liz	Philip and I had put money on the result
Q	No we had not
Liz	He was sure the lady would carry the day. I thought the nation might baulk at a female PM
T	I can remember an odd sense of loneliness when I received the call, which summoned me to the palace
Mags	The audience, at which one receives the Queen's authority to form a government, comes only once in a lifetime. When one is re-elected, one doesn't go. So that first meeting is unique
Liz	She was my eighth
Q	Winston, Sir Anthony,
Liz	Harold M, Sir Alec
Q	Dear Harold W

Liz	Heath –
Q	And Jim Callaghan. He bade me farewell that morning
Liz	It is affecting when they go One doesn't have time to turn around Out goes the last and in comes the next with barely a pause And one has often built up a relationship
Mags	My feelings on the way to the palace –
T	I wasn't thinking about feelings I was thinking there is so much to do. I wanted to get behind that desk in Number Ten and get doing
Mags	My teeth ached from smiling And as we drove through the palace gates I felt almost lifted off the ground As if the hands of fate –
T	I wasn't sentimental
Mags	– were holding me And words were coming to me from my childhood, from our chapel. I wanted to
T	I didn't
Mags	I wanted to give thanks
Liz	It wasn't the first time I'd met Mrs Thatcher, but this was different. Meeting one's PM is like Like meeting the other side of the coin We are both Britain
T	I never said 'there is no such thing as society'
Q	Yes you did. It was in *Woman's Own*
T	I said there is a living tapestry of men and women

Q	You said 'Who is society? There is no such thing' and then you repeated it
T	I said the beauty of that tapestry will depend upon how much each of us is prepared to take responsibility for ourselves
Q	Society is the people
T	Society is a framework for freedom Freedom that gives a man room to breathe To make his own decisions and to chart his own course There is the individual And there is family. There is no such thing as –
Q	No such thing as Britain That's how you sounded
T	It's the idea that the state is society that I reject People in this country feel entitled to state help I reject this entitlement 'I'm homeless, the government must house me – why?
Q	Because one doesn't want homeless people everywhere I would have thought
T	Your Majesty –
Q	This is a big discussion And we're not going to have it now
Mags	I found the monarch's attitude
Liz	I found the Prime Minister's attitude
Mags	Towards the working of government
Liz	Towards the working of monarchy
Mags *and* Liz	
	Absolutely correct

Footman I am a Palace Footman and I'll be leading the
Prime Minister silently and respectfully to her
Majesty the Queen

Mags One enters a different world at the Palace

T Everything is hushed

Footman I am a functionary whose purpose is to serve
To do my job well is to be unnoticed
You may be interested to know that I have a
City and Guilds Diploma in Butlering, and that
the Royal Household is committed to equality
of opportunity

Q Thank you for mentioning that
We're quite modern you see

Footman Prime Minister, the formal kissing of hands –

Mags I know all the protocol. You don't need to tell
me a thing

T Denis was with me

Mags I need Denis

T I want Denis

Mags Where's Denis?

Denis (*entering*) Denis Thatcher
I'm an honest-to-God right-winger and I don't
care who knows it

Mags Denis

Denis Always been a fan of Prince Philip
Big, big admirer
Leader of the pack in this male consort lark;
Absolute model – thought I'd ask him for some
tips

	I reckoned after years and years of PM's wives, He might be grateful for a chap like me
T	Denis came to the door with me
Mags	Why do I suddenly feel like I'm back at school?
Denis	Come on, Boss You'll get on like a house on fire – bound to Just be yourself
Mags	I always am, dear. What a silly thing to say
	Mags curtsies, deeply. She holds it, frozen.
Liz	With my previous Prime Ministers There was a gallantry A mutual letting down of hair
Q	Goodness gracious, what a curtsy
Liz	They were all older than me and each in his own way quite charming. One always hopes for a confidant
	Mags finishes her curtsy.
Liz	Congratulations on your victory, Prime Minister
Mags	Thank you, Your Majesty
T	She's ever so small
Q	She colours her hair
T	We're the same age
Q	Of the same era Formed in the war
T	In every way, we are peers
	Mags kisses Liz's hand.
Liz	Britain's first female leader You must be feeling very pleased

T	Of course I don't notice I'm a woman I regard myself as Prime Minister
Mags	I always say if you want something said, ask a man But if you want something done, ask a woman
Liz	Couldn't agree more
Q	My father never let Prime Ministers sit down
Liz	Please take a seat
	They sit.
Q	We met every week for all the years she was in power
T	Our meetings were private
Liz	We never took notes
Mags	We are the only two who know what was said
Q	Of course stories about clashes
T	Nonsense
Liz	There was never any question
Mags	Stories about clashes
Q	We have got on very well with all of our Prime Ministers
Liz	I was very taken with your prayer on the steps of Number Ten
Mags	Oh yes, St Francis
T	I said

T *and* **Mags**

Where there is discord, may we bring harmony
Where there is error, may we bring truth
Where there is doubt, may we bring faith

Liz	Are you hoping the Conservatives will bring harmony? Because truth and faith are tricky things to supply
Q	I didn't say that. I said –
Liz	What a crush there was on the steps of Number Ten
Mags	Yes
Liz	Journalists and policemen are always so big One finds them enormous They rather crowded you I thought
Mags	Yes, they rather did
Liz	Yet you kept your self-possession
Mags	I am used to the hustle and the bustle
Liz	It'll only get hustlier And bustlier I'm sure
Mags	I shall relish it. I've lived the life of politics since I was twenty-five
Liz	You were a scientist before that?
Mags	First scientist to be PM
Liz	You really are a pioneer
Mags	I was a research chemist for Lyons Developing methods to preserve ice cream And make it fluffier I worked on Mr Whippy Which led the way with hydrogenated fats. Have you heard of it?
Liz	No

Mags	I am of course a barrister as well I qualified four months after my twins were born
Liz	Good gracious
Mags	So between the Party, law, twins and cooking Denis breakfast I have always been very busy
Liz	I am genuinely in awe. I never even went to school
Mags	No
Liz	Your voice changed On the television When they asked about your father
Mags	Well I owe him everything I really do
Liz	One's father shapes one, doesn't he?
Q	I was interested in her family's shop
Mags	It was a very modest home Of course everyone knew deprivation in the war
Liz	Oh yes
Q	I'd done some discreet asking around And her mother, Beatrice – Methodist, terribly devout – Was the daughter of a cloakroom attendant. I thought that was an interesting fact
Mags	My father was very careful with money He abhorred debt – and I have that too
Liz	Your mother must have worked very hard
Mags	Oh yes but of course she was far more domestic. And after I turned fifteen, I had nothing to say to her

Q	Goodness
Liz	I still can't get my mother off the phone
Mags	My father took me out to council meetings and debates He was passionate about politics and about education
Q	Where did she get that accent?
Mags	When I got to Oxford and saw what was being taught – Somerville was very Left and I knew I wouldn't fit in – Something in me thought No, this is wrong, this is wrong No, these consensus economics cap profit You see what we have now is a failed socialist experiment
Q	Everything she said slipped into lecturing mode It was a feature of her conversation
Mags	Socialism
T	Socialism
Mags	Socialism is inimical to freedom. The left-wing slide we have been on leads inexorably to poverty and human bondage
Liz	I'm not a proponent, Prime Minister, but isn't the purpose of socialism to bring people out of poverty?
T	How wonderful; to enter into discourse with her
Mags	Have you read Friedrich Hayek's *The Road to Serfdom*, Ma'am?
Liz	No

Mags He talks about the trend towards socialism as being a break with the whole evolution of western civilisation

Liz Really

Mags You see, our civilisation has grown from foundations of liberty and individuality laid down by the Christians and the Greeks. This individuality is our inheritance. Socialist centralised planning / is a negative to human development. The only way to build a decent world is to improve the level of wealth via the activities of free markets. My father knew this

Q I'm afraid I 'tuned out' – as Charles would say – And when I tuned back in she was talking about her father again

Mags He taught me that you've got to sell your goods every day
It's a constant battle that's never won
It's those who sell who will lift us out of poverty

Liz Yes

T I wasn't sure Her Majesty had understood

Liz I wonder if Number Ten will be like that

Mags How do you mean?

Liz Like living above the shop

Mags Oh yes. I'm sure I shall feel very much at home

Pause.

Liz Prime Minister
One likes to know what's going on
One likes to feel that one's a sort of sponge

	You can come and tell me things
	And some things stay
	And some go out the other ear
	One might occasionally do some good
	And one can put one's point of view
Mags	This is such an honour
Liz	One is unelected, yes
	But one is experienced
T	Disraeli stood in this very room and gave Suez to Victoria
Liz	And perhaps because one cannot publicly express opinion
	One can be a trusted tool
	Especially abroad
T	Winston stood here with her father as the war raged around them
Liz	One's perhaps like an emollient
	One sometimes smoothes the way.
T	And now me
Liz	One cherishes one's service
Mags	Yes, the weight of the cup in the hand
	The shape of the handle, just so – is it Spode?
Q	My God, she hadn't listened
Liz	It's rather an everyday service I think
T	You have no idea what it meant for me
	Meeting you on such an equal footing
Liz	Will you be bringing any pets to Number Ten?
Q	I thought, if she's got a dog we've got a subject
Mags	I believe there is a cat

Q	There was no intimacy with her No letting down of hair
T	You are my Queen I am your subject The first move towards a close relationship Could not have come from me
Mags	You never made it
Q	You didn't hear it
Liz	You hadn't listened
Denis	Margaret had always adored the Queen, absolutely revered her. We stood in the crowd cheering at her Coronation. Seemed sad to me she came out so deflated
T	On my way back to Number Ten A thought stayed there insistently Despite my every effort to dispel it
Denis	Felt a bit like the grocer's daughter did you, love?
Mags	Not at all I felt as soon as I had left the room Her Majesty would shake me off – with a laugh
Liz	You're quite wrong
Q	There was nothing remotely funny about you
T	I had worked so hard for my achievements Her Majesty's were birthrights
Q	I have to accept that here I am And this is my fate
T	Fate has nothing to do with me It is all discipline and enterprise

THREE: SPANKING

Liz I notice the Prime Minister didn't eat the biscuits. Let's try her with a sponge next time

Footman Very good, Ma'am. May I ask you a question?

Q and Liz allow it.

Is it different because this Prime Minister is a woman?

Liz It is different because this Prime Minister is Mrs Thatcher

Footman (*to T and Mags*) Prime Minister. May I ask you a question?

T Of course you may

Footman When you said that socialism was inimical to freedom, what did you mean?

T I meant that –

Mags Socialism is the philosophy of failure, the creed of ignorance, and the gospel of envy. Its inherent virtue is the equal sharing of misery

T Winston Churchill said that and I agree with every word

Mags One cannot have liberty without economic liberty and we shall attain it with our monetarist policies and our strong stance against the trade unions. May I offer you our manifesto?

Footman Thank you.
Don't you think you should have something about the other side?

Mags They lost

T   They are utterly discredited and that is thanks
to me

Footman Only there's a generation that don't know what
they were about

T   Yes, aren't you lucky?

Footman But the Labour Party –

Mags May we push on?

Denis Prince Philip and I
House on fire
But Margaret was struggling

Mags Your Majesty, I have a query
A slightly awkward one
About our wardrobe
It has occurred to me that when we attend the
same event, our outfits may present complications
For example, one wouldn't want to wear a
similar colour or a clashing one

Liz I never notice what anyone else wears

Mags One wouldn't like to upstage

Liz I shouldn't worry about that

Pause.

Mags Do you have a lady, Your Majesty
One of your ladies
That perhaps my lady could speak to?

Q The way she said 'Your Majesty' grated.
Why couldn't she just call me Ma'am?

Liz I have Bobo
Bobo organises all my clothes

Mags I have Crawfie
Crawfie does everything for me

She turns me out every morning looking spanking.
Would it be acceptable if Crawfie were to ask Bobo? . . .

Footman The butler who trained me has worked in the Palace for thirty-five years. He said you overheard all sorts of things and that your job is to forget them. Then he told me some of the things he'd forgotten. The Queen used to call Mrs Thatcher 'that bloody woman'

Q No one from the Palace ever said that

T Yes they did
You and your sister did
You think things didn't get back to Number Ten
But I heard everything
I knew exactly what you thought of me

The Queen ignores her, shaking invisible hands.

Q One has so many people to meet
So much to do

T I never held an unkind thought about you
I am your most loyal subject

Q How do you do?
Yes, community service is so important

T Don't ignore me please

Q Two mayors? How lovely

Mags The Queen is a continuum
A line drawn through time
From the dawn of England to the present day
Her family symbolises all that is perfect and proper in British life
She is

Liz	Completely useless
	That's the impression one got
	She thought we were fit for nothing more than
	shaking hands
Q	Oh, Barbados? Terribly nice place
T	I felt a tremendous desire to protect the Queen
Liz	One had been patronised before, of course
	But it was worse being patronised by Mrs
	Thatcher
Q	A hairdresser, really?

FOUR: DANCING AT LUSAKA

Liz   I soon gave her proof of my usefulness.
        Rhodesia –

Q   Now Zimbabwe –

Liz   – had been a thorn in our side for fifteen years

Footman Shall I fill them in on the history, Ma'am?

Liz   Do you have to? I don't want this to get dull
        and there's a lot to get through before the
        interval

T   We don't need an interval

Q   What?

T   I'd like to go right through

Q ˙   But I enjoy the interval
        Sometimes it's the best part of the play

Liz   In my opinion, the people of Rhodesia deserve a
        fair election

Mags   In my opinion, the existing government of Rhodesia, whatever its flaws, is the only one that won't ruin the country

T   It was our first real disagreement

Q   Of course it wasn't. We never disagreed

Footman   The young people might need the background, Ma'am. I can cover it in a sentence or two

Q   Oh very well

Footman   Rhodesia – now Zimbabwe – was ruled by a white minority led by Ian Smith. It refused to hold fair elections and there had been an escalating guerrilla war for several years as a result. The Zimbabwean Patriotic Front was led by the hugely popular Robert Mugabe, who was currently harboured by Zambia

Q   Thank you. Very concise

Liz   The people deserve democracy

Mags   The Zimbabwean Patriotic Front is Marxist. Marxists do not respect democracy

Denis   I knew Rhodesia very well from my days at Burmah Oil. And if the blackies got in the whole place would go down the bloody plughole. And with it, a great hairball of British interests and British trade

Liz   The Heads of Commonwealth conference is in Lusaka this year

Footman   Lusaka is the capital of Zambia

Liz   I think it's an ideal opportunity for us to get all the parties round the table

T	*Us?* Is the Queen suddenly a member of Her Majesty's government?
Mags	Your Majesty, your government has grave concerns for your safety in Lusaka. We strongly advise you not to go
Liz	You advise me not to go?
Mags	It has been bombed. It is unsafe
Liz	I have only ever missed one Heads of Commonwealth meeting and that's because I was having Andrew
Mags	Your Majesty, Kenneth Kaunda of Zambia is thick as thieves with Mugabe and the guerrillas. / It is dangerous
Liz	We've known Kenneth Kaunda for years – he wouldn't let anything happen to me
Mags	Your government is responsible for your safety; you must let your government decide
Liz	So you are *telling* the monarch not to go?
Mags	I am merely trying to protect you, Your Majesty
Q	We were jolly well going
Liz	And if anyone tries to stop us there'll be a whole song and dance about it I can tell you
T	Of course, if the Queen wanted to go then the Queen had to go and all the security had to be provided
Q	You were the one who needed protecting You were too green to see it I knew I could be useful To you and to Britain So obviously I was going

Footman Would it be helpful if I changed parts now, Ma'am?
I could stop being Palace Footman
And play Kenneth Kaunda, President of Zambia

Q Can you do that?

Footman Yes, I'll just go and prepare
And when I come back, I will be him

Actor 2 smoothly changes his glasses.

Carrington
Prepare? I'm Peter Carrington, Foreign Secretary

Actor 2 exits.

T You're not Peter Carrington

Carrington
Yes, for the moment I am

T You're Denis

Carrington
Yes I was, but now I'm Peter Carrington

T How can you be Peter Carrington when you're Denis?

Carrington
I'm representing Peter Carrington
Just for a moment or two

T Why?

Carrington
Because I'm responsible for the Lancaster House Agreement. It gave Zimbabwe peace and democracy

T Are you Denis or not?

Actor 2 No, I'm not

| T | How dare you |
| | How dare you attempt to impersonate him |

T exits.

| Actor 2 | Look I'm playing several roles here – I mean, some of them have only got one line and others are horrible, thin caricatures, but times are hard and it's a job. I don't want to offend anyone. All right? |
| | I am currently Foreign Secretary and Minister for Overseas Development; Peter Carrington |

| Q | He goes on to be Secretary General of NATO |

| Liz | Quite a gentleman, Peter |

| Mags | Yes, you hail from the days when the Conservative Party was run by men from Eton |

Carrington
Of course you change all that – for a while

| Mags | What if I want you to be Denis again? |

| Actor 2 | I am employed to be anyone you need |

| Mags | Thank you. I shall go and make that clear |

She exits.

| Q | I have always loved Africa. |

| Liz | My first trip abroad was to South Africa |

| Q | I can honestly say it was one of the happiest times of my life |

| Liz | It was just after the war and there was such a feeling of hope and renewal in the air |

| Q | There were picnics and big game hunts |

| Liz | And coloured balls |

Q   On my twenty-first birthday I made a speech

Carrington
            Ma'am, no one who heard it will ever forget

Q   I felt the whole Empire was listening

Mags   (*entering, with T*) Come on, Peter. We're going
            to Lusaka

Liz   'I declare before you all, that my whole life,
            whether it be long or short, shall be devoted
            to your service and the service of our great
            Imperial family, to which we all belong . . .'

Carrington
            It was most affecting
            To hear the young princess
            Take on that great burden
            With such a sweet pure voice

T   There's a whole generation of men, Peter among
            them, who went through the war and are quite
            batty about the Queen

Carrington
            We would have lain down our lives for her –

Mags   Are you coming, Peter?

Carrington
            And still would

Mags   Peter – I'm already on the plane

Kaunda (*entering*) I'm Kenneth Kaunda, Father of Zambia

Q   That's very good

Kaunda I'm about halfway through my twenty-seven
            years of rule, during which time I abuse
            democracy and amass a huge personal fortune.
            But that's another story.

When we Commonwealth heads of government meet, we are all equal under the Queen. In other words, the British government is just one of many

T   Purgatory

Kaunda The Queen is like a mother confessor to us all
            A very down-to-earth person
            Always asking her incisive questions
            Really, she is an icon

Q   I arrived in Lusaka before Mrs Thatcher. I was determined to smooth her way

Liz   Kenneth, I want to know all about the Zimbabwean Patriotic Front. You let them train here; you give them arms – what are they like?

Kaunda Her Majesty never wastes time

Liz   What about this Mugabe chap? I'm hearing such conflicting things

Kaunda You know you can trust my opinion, Ma'am

Mags   On the plane, I was sick with dread

Carrington
            Margaret, the Americans support free elections. The UN supports free elections. Frankly, our position is becoming untenable

Mags   But I cannot back down. This is my first outing on the international stage and –

Carrington
            And you can be seen to be listening

Mags   Peter, when one knows one is right, that is very hard

Carrington
>The thing that people forget is how cautious
>Margaret was
>She was very careful
>And she was persuadable
>In the early years at least

T   By the end of the flight my address was written

Mags   I should like to make it clear that the British
           government is wholly committed to genuine
           black majority rule in Rhodesia

Carrington
>Zimbabwe

Mags   Zimbabwe

Q   Thanks to Peter, the lady had turned

Carrington
>Margaret put on a large pair of dark glasses
>I said what on earth are those for?

Mags   I am absolutely certain that when I land at
           Lusaka they are going to throw acid in my face

Kaunda Welcome to Lusaka, Prime Minister
            I'm sure you will find it a very convivial place

Liz   I had taken Kenneth aside
            I told him you'd be nervous
            Pointed out that you were new

Kaunda I have great love and respect for Britain's
            Queen. So I made her Prime Minister welcome.
            And in spite of everything I'd heard, I found the
            Iron Lady quite conversable

Mags   It turned out that Kenneth Kaunda was not as
            black as he'd been painted

Q   Did you really say that?

T   Yes, what of it?

Carrington
            Margaret's speech was very well received. With
            British support, a free Zimbabwe was on the
            agenda

Kaunda   The atmosphere at the final reception was quite
            extraordinary

Liz   My work behind the scenes paid off
            Mrs Thatcher was accepted by the African
            leaders
            And I swear she began to enjoy herself

Mags   Crawfie had packed something special and I
            thought well by golly, I'm going to make a
            splash

T   No I didn't

Kaunda   Mrs Thatcher's dress was a dramatic shade of
            lime with a pineapple motif. Her blond hair
            shone through the crowd
            Margaret, may I have this dance?

            They dance.

Q   Denis was overheard asking the New Zealand
            High Commissioner

Denis   What do you think those fuzzy-wuzzies are up
            to?

Liz   I made it known I was available for a dance

            Denis and Liz are dancing.

Denis   The Queen certainly kept her cool in the
            tropical heat. In fact she was quite chilly

Liz   Not quite the Gay Gordons, is it?

Mags	And so Rhodesia expired and Zimbabwe was born
T	Has Carrington gone?
Denis	He took the rap for the Falklands, old girl. Resigned when the Argies barged in
Mags	He was very good over Rhodesia. He brought it off
Denis	Yes but he didn't dance with Kaunda
Mags	I should hope not
Denis	You did – and that's what turned the trick
Kaunda	I'm being forgotten here. My diplomacy brought all the parties to the table
Mags	I doubt if that's what history will say
T	The atmosphere was very special at Lusaka And that was due to the Queen
Q	Twenty-three years later she publicly expressed her gratitude
Mags	I've always loved to dance. We had American servicemen in Grantham during the war. They were so glamorous
Liz	Oh yes
Mags	And I begged and begged to go dancing. My father wouldn't hear of it
Liz	We crept out on VE Day, my sister and I, with some officers we were friendly with; went into the crowd incognito – dancing on the street
Mags	Did you really?
Liz	Of course they recognised us. But the crowd was lovely

T	I was deeply gratified when she shared things with me
Mags	I cried when they brought down the Union Jack in Rhodesia
Liz	Did you?
Mags	I thought 'the poor Queen . . .'
Liz	Why?
Mags	Doesn't it grieve you? The demise of the Empire?
Liz	The Commonwealth has more value to me. Every nation is there by choice
T	I felt pain for Britain's decline To see how low we'd sunk in the world's esteem
Q	Not everything was in decline I for one thought it was wonderful How many schools and hospitals I'd opened in my reign
T	We were an economic snail An international nonentity
Q	Society had never been more equal
Mags	Someone had to stop the rot Someone had to change it all

FIVE: BOMBS I

T	If I had my way, Irish citizens in the UK would lose their right to vote and they'd be subject to the same immigration laws as everybody else
Mags	I never said that
T	But crikey I thought it

Q	Mrs Thatcher had lost her friend and mentor Airey Neave in an IRA bomb blast just before she was elected
Mags	He was one of freedom's warriors. No one knew how great a man he was except those nearest to him We must not let the people who got him triumph
Liz	Her voice cracked as she spoke of him
T	We had barely been back from Lusaka a week when the IRA murdered eighteen of Our Boys at Warrenpoint in a hideous ambush
Mags	At the security briefing one of the officers presented me with a torn epaulette. I said what is this? It was all that remained of his friend
T	Carnage
Liz	On the same day, at his home in Sligo, our cousin Louis Mountbatten –
Q	Dickie to those who knew him –
Liz	– set off with his family in his boat, the *Shadow Five*
Adams	Gerry Adams, Sinn Fein. What the IRA did to Mountbatten is what Mountbatten had been doing all his life to other people; and with his war record I don't think he could have objected to dying in what was clearly a war situation. He knew what he was doing, coming to our country. In my opinion, the IRA achieved its objective: people started paying attention to what was happening in Ireland
Q	The explosion was violent in the extreme. It was heard across the bay over two miles away

Nothing but flotsam remained of the *Shadow Five*

Liz It was terrible for Philip in particular
Dickie was his uncle
Had been like a father to him

Q Two children died in that blast
Boys aged fourteen and fifteen

Liz You didn't phone me

Q She didn't phone

Mags Because I was new you see and I didn't know
whether one telephoned the Queen or not
Normally, you go through the system

Q Members of my family had died

Liz And I had to phone you

T Of course I went to Ulster straight away
And I got doing

Mags We put a thousand more men in the RUC

T I never ever compromised with terror
I told them compromise? That is out

Mags That is out

T That is out
I wanted troops on every street

Mags I would root out

T I would vanquish

Mags Crush

T Pulverise the IRA

Mags And if they protest

T If they protest

Ron	The ten most dangerous words in the English language are, 'Hi, I'm from the Government and I'm here to help'

Mags *and* **T**
Ron

Q	One has seen many Presidents come and go And from this peculiar position One can see that power rests in the office

Liz	Not in the individual

SIX: THE REAGANS ARE COMING

Ron	There were two guys in Moscow waiting in line for vodka and one them says, 'This line is too long; I've had enough. I'm going into the Kremlin and I'm going to kill Brezhnev.' So off he goes and after about an hour he comes back. And the other guy says, 'So did you kill him?' and he says, 'No that line was even longer.'
T	Ron was even funnier than Denis
Mags	The first time I set eyes on Ronald Reagan –
T	Apart from on the screen of course
Mags	– was in the Royal Albert Hall in 1969. There was the Governor of California Speaking as if it were just to me
Ron	We're at war with the most dangerous enemy that has ever faced mankind in his long climb from the swamp to the stars: Communism
Mags	I knew in an instant that here was a visionary Not only that –

34

T	He was gorgeous I'm sorry but why not say it?
Mags	Never said it, never thought it
T	Who can deny it? Not even Denis
Ron	Someone once said to me, 'How can an actor be president?' I said, 'How can a president not be an actor?'
Q	Have we seen any of his films?
Liz	*The Cattle Queen of Montana*, that was one of his
Q	Oh yes, we liked that
Liz	We liked the horses
Q	Didn't he have a bit part in *Dark Victory*?
T	I've no idea
Liz	He did. He flirts with Bette Davis before she gets the brain tumour
Mags	Long before he was elected, I used to cherish copies of his speeches in my bag –
Ron	Ladies and gentlemen, this is my wife
Nancy	Hello, how do you do? I'm Nancy Reagan
Mags	The First Lady
Nancy	We first met Maggie and Denis back when Ron was fighting for his nomination And those two? They hit it off straight away
Ron	She had a lot of spunk
Mags	We'd talk half the night about the dangers of big government

Nancy	They even had a conversation that went something like
	Wouldn't it be great if we two ruled the world?
	And then lo and behold –
T	I was the first foreign leader to visit him in Washington after his inauguration
Liz	No you weren't. The Koreans were
Mags	We in Britain stand with you
T	America's successes will be our successes
Mags	Your problems will be our problems
T	And when you look for friends we will be there
Ron	In a dangerous world, one element goes without question: Britain and America stand side by side
Mags	We must be free or die who speak the tongue that Shakespeare spake
Ron	Margaret, I believe a real friendship exits between us

Mags *and* T

> So do I, Ron

Nancy	Dinner at the British Embassy was a warm and beautiful occasion
	Bob Hope was there; all sorts of wonderful people
Liz	I hear she's notoriously brittle
Mags	Who?
Liz	The First Lady
Mags	She's very slim, yes
Liz	Apparently it's her hustling that's propelled him into the White House – and now that she's

there, I've heard she's knocking down walls and throwing out all the china

Q   I love gossip

Mags   She is undertaking some refurbishments

Q   Why wouldn't you gossip?
You knew I wasn't going to tell anyone

Liz   Well, I would have told Philip

Q   And my sister

Liz   And probably Mummy and Anne

Mags   The First Lady adores the President
She's always at his side
I'm sure he relies on her

Liz   I heard she sees an astrologer about absolutely everything. One of these people who won't get their hair cut unless the moon's in the right place

Mags   We haven't discussed astrology, Your Majesty

Q   Oh, it was such hard work

Liz   Do you not feel it's a bit of a performance with them?
They are both actors, you know

Ron   When I got shot in March '81, Margaret's letter of concern was top of the pile

Nancy   I cannot describe what I went through on that day

Ron   You don't have to, Nancy

Nancy   Yes I do, Ronnie. Because people need to know. A crazy man called John Hinkley, was obsessed with a teenaged actress called Jodie Foster – I'm not kidding – and he thought he would please

her somehow if he shot my husband.
He let off six bullets

Ron   He was a lousy shot. Only one of them got me

Nancy   It stopped in his lung, an inch away from his heart

Ron   I was a lucky man. The surgeons who operated on me were all Republicans

Mags   His wit, even in such adversity. That showed real mettle

Nancy   You can be one of the premier people in the world, protected round the clock by servicemen and bang –
All it takes is one lunatic with a gun

Mags   It was sobering

Liz   Very sobering

Q   Because of the shooting, The President was unable to attend Charles and Diana's wedding that summer

Nancy   I wasn't going to let him travel

Q   But luckily the First Lady came

Nancy   It was a fairytale event. Diana was so beautiful
And no one does a Royal occasion like the British
I missed Ronnie terribly

T   Yes, we all did

Nancy   I was in London five days and I had eighteen different engagements

Q   One of them was a polo match
She came to meet Charles and Diana

Nancy   He was such a delightful, earnest young man
And I could see even then that Diana had a
stunning personality
This was the romance of all times

Liz   I'd driven there in my jeep
Headscarf on
Mrs Reagan arrived in a cavalcade – of how
many cars?

T   Six

Mags   One just for her hats I think

Liz   Really, Mrs Thatcher, was that a joke?

Mags   No

Liz   It was – you were being funny

Mags   It just slipped out

Q   She actually made a joke. It was a first. I thought
she had no sense of humour whatsoever

Mags   I didn't mean anything. I admire the First Lady

Liz   But you've got to admit that the sixth car was a
bit much

Mags   Thank goodness for such a lovely wedding,
Your Majesty
It's transformed a horrible summer

SEVEN: THE GUNS OF BRIXTON

Ron   Nancy must have hit it off with Queen Elizabeth
because that winter we received an official
invitation to Windsor Castle. No US president
had ever stayed there before

Actor 1   I'm sorry but is that it about the summer of '81?

T	I beg your pardon?
Actor 1	Are we moving on from the summer of '81?
Mags	Yes
Actor 1	You don't want to mention the riots?
T	No
Actor 1	The race riots that flared up all over the country?
Q	Oh one found them very distressing and one said so in one's Christmas message
T	You're Nancy Reagan
Mags	Nancy Reagan was never concerned with unlawful rioting in British cities I can assure you of that
Q	May I refer you to my Christmas message? My feelings are made very clear
Actor 1	I just feel there's some massive omissions here – The huge job losses; unemployment leapt by a million in one year The unrest in Northern Ireland The hunger strikes –
Actor 2	Look – it's not our gig, OK?
Actor 1	I'm just saying that if you miss out the riots and all the unrest, people – you know, like younger people – might think nothing else happened in 1981 apart from the royal wedding and – Bucks Fizz winning the Eurovision
Actor 2	How did you know about Bucks Fizz?
Actor 1	My research. I Wiki'd the eighties
Actor 2	You Wiki'd the eighties?

Q	One's Christmas message is the only major speech of the year that is written without government intervention
Liz	This Christmas, we should remember especially the people of Northern Ireland who are attempting to live ordinary lives in times of strain and conflict; the unemployed who are trying to maintain their self-respect without work and to care for their families; and those from other parts of the Commonwealth who have come to Britain to make new lives but have not yet found themselves fully accepted
Actor 1	That must have really shaken things up
Q	Listen
Liz	Governments now regard it as their duty to try to protect their people, through social services, from the worst effects of illness, bereavement, joblessness and disability
Q	How much clearer could I have made things?
Actor 2	Look, I don't think you should be disrespectful Constitutionally she's not allowed to state her opinions
Actor 1	I'm not being disrespectful I'm just saying that in the midst of all that royal carriage big dress Diana wedding stuff The whole country was boiling with rage
Mags	The whole country? The whole country?
Actor 1	Well, people on the street
Mags	Which people on the street? How many?
Actor 1	Crowds, you know

Mags	How many in each crowd?
Actor 1	Well, in Brixton there was about five thousand
Mags	Five thousand yobs? – The whole country?
T	(*to the actors*) I'd like to remind you what you're here for and whose company you're in. Her Majesty was shot at during the trooping of the colour, two weeks before the Prince of Wales' wedding and did she go on about it? No she did not She passed it by without a word Such is her dignity Such is her courage
Q	One doesn't want to be standing here all night
Mags	We choose what is spoken about here and if you don't like it you can get on your bike
	Pause.
Actor 1	I'm just saying. But in a stroke of casting genius I've been asked to play Nancy Reagan – so I'll play Nancy Reagan
Mags	I fell over myself to be useful to Ron I would give him my careful advice at any hour of the day or night
Ron	Margaret certainly never held back with her advice
T	I would have guided his finger as it hovered over NATO's button I'd have made sure he held firm
Mags	But the first time I really needed him He let me down
Q	Can we skip this bit?

T   Pardon?

Q   We've been here aeons and we're not even
        though your first term

T   Your Majesty, how can you even suggest it?

EIGHT: ISLANDS IN THE STREAM

Ron   When Al Haig told me that Argentina had
        invaded the Falkland Islands, I said where in the
        name of ding-dong are they?

Nancy   No he didn't

Ron   A little ice-cold bunch of land down in the
        South Atlantic, of no strategic value to anyone

Mags   On the 2nd of April 1982
        Argentina, led by General Galtieri and his
        Junta –

Q   We're not going through the whole thing, are
        we?

Liz   We don't need a blow-by-blow account

T   I'm sorry?

Q   It's been gone over again and again in all sorts
        of other places and I don't want to trudge
        through it here

Mags   Three days later,
        With UN approval
        A task force set sail from Portsmouth

Q   She's ignoring me

Mags   There would be no negotiation till these bullies
        had got off

Q   Did you see that?

T	That's when Ron should have stepped up
Q	Totally ignoring me
Mags	He should have said I support you one hundred per cent We are side by side This invasion is an outrage against democracy
Q	She's just going to carry on, isn't she? I might as well not be here
T	Ron sat on the fence When I needed him most
Mags	He sent a jet-lagged proposal Suggesting we negotiate
Nancy	I think you Brits forget how close we are to Latin America
Ron	There was a lot of Soviet-funded trouble going on down there – and Galtieri was no Communist
T	Negotiate? I said no
Mags	No, Ron
T	Absolutely not
Mags	You're asking me to lie down And let naked aggression walk all over me I am a not a doormat And you may not wipe your feet
Liz	May I interrupt you for a moment?
T	Of course
Liz	I was directly involved in the South Atlantic war Firstly, as head of the armed forces
T	Oh yes

Liz	Then, as sovereign of the country that was being invaded
T	Yes, of course, but that's all titular isn't it
Liz	And I was mother of a combatant
Q	My son Andrew was out there
Liz	Your Cabinet tried to give him a desk job But I insisted, insisted that he went Countless other mothers were waving off their sons Why should I be spared?
T	We were very grateful for your sacrifice It was a battle of good over evil
Ron	Margaret, you've got to try the diplomatic initiative
Mags	I had an absolute clarity of purpose I knew I had to hold my nerve
T	And I was put, by Ron, on an equal footing with the Junta
Ron	We decided in the end on a pro-UK tilt
Mags	A tilt
T	Ron came through with a tilt
Mags	I felt personally let down
Q	You'd think Wouldn't you That she did the whole thing by herself That there was no one else involved
Liz	Well, Andrew was on the HMS *Invincible* And I can tell you there were a lot of people involved

Mags I was stricken at our losses
They caused me acute distress
I wrote personally to the families of all the men
who died

Liz There it is again – I, me, I

T This is all about taking the salute, isn't it?

Q Nonsense

T This is because when it was over I took the
salute and not you

Q I have kept silent on that subject, always

Ron We could see that a certain amount of damage
had been done to our special relationship

Q So thank heavens for me

Liz When the Reagans visited Windsor, the conflict
was still at its height

Nancy The Queen was so thoughtful
She showed us up to our room herself
And you should have seen the little things she'd
put out for us
There were letters from Abraham Lincoln
There was a note from George the Third saying
'America is lost to us!'

Ron I found that very poignant

Nancy And there was the sweetest letter from Her
Majesty's parents, written when they were
visiting President Roosevelt. It described a picnic
they'd been on, where the King had eaten a hot
dog for the first time in his life

Liz For the only time in his life

Nancy I was knocked out by Windsor Castle

Liz	Yes that's rather the idea
Mags	The battle for Goose Green was raging
Ron	The Queen had suggested we have a ride. Now, I was worried I can tell you; At home in Santa Barbara I'd just pull on some jeans And leap on, you know, John Wayne style –
Mags	There was vicious hand-to-hand fighting on Mount Tumbledown –
Ron	But the last thing I wanted to come over as, was a cowboy –
T	They sank the *Atlantic Conveyor* –
Q	And who was first on the scene to lift off the survivors? Andrew, in his Sea King
Mags	I was existing on one or two hours sleep
T	I felt intensely, intensely alive
Nancy	We wrote to the palace and asked what the President should wear
Liz	Boots, breeches and a sweater No need to be formal
Nancy	In the end we decided on something Old Hollywood Beautiful sports jacket over an open-necked shirt
Liz	We rode Burmese, our favourite
Nancy	Ron looked so elegant So did the Queen, in a charming head scarf
Ron	You know, she was in charge of that animal
Liz	Those images were beamed around the world From Moscow to Buenos Aires

Q	Britain and America side by side in in perfect harmony
Liz	It's marvellous, the benefits of a good ride
Mags	Of course the important thing about Ron's visit was his speech to Parliament, when he talked about putting Marxism on the ash-heap of history
Q	No one remembers that
T	Four days later The Union Jack was flying over Port Stanley Right had prevailed Victory was ours
Mags	Enoch Powell stood up in the house and he said:

Pause.

Actor 2	That's you
Actor 1	No it's not
Actor 2	Yes it is
Actor 1	I made sure at the audition; I don't have to do it
Actor 2	Well, it's you. I'm still Reagan
Actor 1	I'm not Enoch Powell
Q	Shall we move on?
Mags	Enoch Powell stood up in the house and he said:
Actor 1	I'm not doing it
Mags	I beg your pardon?
Actor 1	I'm just not
T	Then you're very poor value for money
Mags	You yourself pointed out current levels of unemployment. If you don't want this job –

Actor 1 I do

Mags Then I suggest you get on with it

T Enoch said:

Powell Her substance is ferrous metal of the highest quality
Of exceptional tensile strength
Resistant to wear and tear
Usable for all national purposes

Mags I agree with everything the gentleman has said

Q Gloriana, the papers called her
Boadicea in pearls

Liz I'd spent those weeks
Along with countless other mothers
Agonising for the safety of my favourite son –

Q I have no favourites

T All right, I took the salute
It felt right at the time and Our Boys wanted it
They wanted me
I had brought them safely home
Restoring Britain's honour and your flag

Pause.

Mags It's done
If I'd known you'd be this upset
I'd have –

Liz You'd have what, Prime Minister?

Mags I know my son wasn't out there but the
following year when Mark got lost in the desert
and I didn't know where he was for four whole
days, I got an inkling of what you must have felt

Pause.

	Are you freezing me out?

Liz is silent.

T	She froze me out for weeks over that salute
Q	Nonsense
Liz	The following year we visited the Reagans in California

NINE: CALIFORNIA DREAMING

T	I won the next election with a landslide
Q	California please
Ron	We invited Queen Elizabeth to our home, Rancho del Cielo
Nancy	We threw them a Hollywood dinner. We invited movie stars; Julie Andrews was there, Rod Stewart sang
Ron	I figured she'd like a ride, American style And where better to provide it?
Mags	If Ronald Reagan knew If he knew what I really thought of him His lazy intellect, His mawkish sentiment His fumbling with briefs It would damage our interests irrevocably
T	On one thing, Ron was clear
Mags	The evil of socialism
T	I held on to that one thing
Mags	I brought him Gorbachev I gave Ron the Soviet empire in a golf cart

T	To anyone who says that my diplomacy was poor I give them this: we ended communism. We brought down that wall
Mags	The first time I met Mikhail Gorbachev, I knew this was a man we could do business with
Actor 1	Hold on, what year are we in?
T	1985
Actor 1	Are you going to miss out the government's decision to allow America to site its Cruise missiles on British soil?
Mags	Yes
Actor 1	What about the women protesting at Greenham Common?
Mags	Eurgh
Actor 1	Or the huge CND marches?
T	They weren't huge
Actor 1	What about the miners' strike? Are you going to miss that out too?
T	I'd be glad to talk about the miners' strike. Let's talk about the miners' strike
Mags	Where's Michael Heseltine? He was useful
Hesel	I'm Michael Heseltine Most handsome member of the cabinet
Mags	Hezza
Hesel	We knew there was a confrontation coming. The most meticulous planning had been put in place. We'd been stockpiling coal for years

Mags	There'd be no power cuts on my watch
Hesel	Arthur Scargill was teased on to the worst battle plan at the worst possible time for him – and the rest is history
T	We planned it like a military campaign
Mags	We had to fight the enemy without in the Falklands. But the enemy within is more difficult And more dangerous to liberty
Liz	Have you ever been down a mine, Mrs Thatcher? I have I thought it was a dark and dangerous place to work I was deeply impressed by the men who laboured there. I've spoken with a lot of miners and their wives
Mags	Then you are very knowledgeable –
Liz	And never, at any time Have I found them to be The enemy within
T	We had to win. Anything else was unthinkable
Q	(*to Actor 1*) Perhaps you'd like to be a miner?
Actor 1	(*still dressed as Nancy*) Can I go and get changed?
T	We're not hanging around whilst you cover yourself in coal dust
Mags	They are behaving as a mob And we have no choice but to treat them as a mob
Liz	I don't like the way you're pitting my police force against them. They fought side by side

during the war and it upsets me how you have divided them

Mags   I have not divided them. Arthur Scargill has divided them

Actor 2   Shall I be Scargill?

Mags *and* **T**
    No

T   The only helpful thing that Arthur Scargill ever did was neglect to hold a strike ballot. That was very helpful. Very helpful indeed

Mags   It revealed his undemocratic soul

Scargill   We've had riot shields, we've had riot gear, we've had police on horseback charging into our people; we've had people hit with truncheons and people kicked to the ground

Mags   You are stepping over the mark

Scargill   The intimidation and the brutality that has been displayed are something of a Latin American state

Mags   (*to Scargill*) He is the dictator
He is the general

T   His real aim is the breakdown of law and order and the destruction of democratic parliamentary government

Liz   Neither would back down an inch

Q   When one thinks about it, they were very similar

Liz   I felt particularly sorry for the miners' wives, as the strike dragged through the winter

Mags   It is up to the miners' wives to tell the miners to be sensible

Actor 1 Did you really say that?

Mags No husband of mine would have gone around shaming the country in that lawless way; picketing here, rioting there

Actor 1 But you were going to close all the mines

Mags All the *unproductive* mines

Q It was a whole year of strife

Mags I welcome strife
I welcome it
In the cause of making Britain great again

Q And in the end, the miners were beaten

Liz Some of the wives handed them carnations at the pit gates as they returned to work; a flower which symbolises the hero. I thought that rather affecting

Actor 2 In 1983, Britain had one hundred and seventy deep coalmines; now there is one

Mags It is simply bad housekeeping to keep unprofitable pits open

Actor 2 Whole communities lost their work. It was a tragedy; it was heartbreaking

T Who said that?

Actor 2 No one important

T Is that your own private opinion?

Mags It is. It's his own opinion.
Would you tell me whose opinion these people have paid good money to hear?

Actor 2 Her Majesty's opinion

T	And?
Actor 2	And your opinion
T	What does your opinion count for here?
Mags	What does your opinion count for?
Actor 2	It destroyed more than people's livelihoods. It destroyed the whole idea of the dignity of labour
Mags	Have these people paid to hear that?
Actor 2	No
T	Then what does it count for? I'm sorry, I didn't hear that
Actor 2	Nothing
Q	I'd like an interval now, please
T	We don't need an interval Whoever ordered an interval they can cancel it
Mags	There's too much to do
Q	Don't you want an interval Prime Minister?
T *and* **Mags**	No
	Pause.
Q	There will now be a fifteen minute interval

TEN: THE GAP

Actor 1 Why don't you tell them what you were telling me, back in the dressing room?

Actor 2 No

Actor 1 Why not?

Actor 2 I don't want to

Actor 1 What are you scared of?

Actor 2 I'm not scared

Actor 1 You're being a chicken

Actor 2 I'm not a chicken.
What's history for you is life lived for me
I can't heave it into my mouth like you can
It is not easy to talk about those years. Not in
public anyway

Actor 1 Go on, before they come back

Actor 2 OK. My parents loved the Tories, I loathed them

Actor 1 Why in particular

Actor 2 You've seen Act One.
It was their hypocrisy I hated most. They
allowed homophobia to thrive. They passed
legislation that was blatantly prejudiced –
Section 28 for example

Actor 1 What was that?

Actor 2 If I was to tell you publicly, I'd be in breach of
Section 28

Actor 1 Seriously?

Actor 2 Who are you playing in this half?

Actor 1 Michael Shea – he's the Queen's press secretary

Actor 2 I'm Murdoch – got a line of Prince Philip; look out for that one, folks –

Actor 1 And I'm Kinnock

Actor 2 Are you?

Actor 1 Yes

Actor 2 I wanted to be Kinnock

Actor 1 Did you?

Actor 2 I can do a good Kinnock

Actor 1 Yes, but he's in my contract

Actor 2 Have you got his 'I warn you' speech?

Actor 1 No

Actor Oh what a shame, you should have the 'I warn you' speech. It's bloody good

Actor 1 I know but he said it in '83
We've already gone past it

Actor 2 I warn you that you will have pain – when healing and relief depend upon payment

Actor 1 I'm Kinnock

Actor 2 I warn you that you will have ignorance – when learning is a privilege and not a right

Actor 1 You can't just take my part

Actor 2 I warn you that you will have poverty –

Actor 1 Do you want a Kinnock-off?

Actor 2   When pensions slip –

Actor 1   Cos I'll give you one

Actor 2   And benefits are whittled away –

Actor 1   By a government that won't pay in an economy that can't pay

Actor 2   I warn you that you will be cold

Actor 1   When fuel charges are used as a tax system that the rich don't notice and the poor can't afford

Actor 2   I warn you that you must not expect work

Actor 1   I warn you not to go into the streets alone after dark

Actor 2   Or into the streets in large crowds of protest in the light

Actor 1   I warn you that you will be quiet

Both   When the curfew of fear and the gibbet of unemployment make you obedient

Actor 1   I warn you that you will borrow less – when credit, loans and mortgages are refused to people on your melting income

Mags and T have entered.

Actor 2   If Margaret Thatcher wins on Thursday, I warn you not to be ordinary

Actor 1   I warn you not to be young

Actor 2   I warn you not to fall ill

Actor 1   I warn you not to grow old

The Actors notice Thatcher. Pause. Actor 2 puts Denis's glasses on

T	Denis
Denis	Hello love
T	Come away from him. Have you had some refreshments?
Denis	Yes, fully tanked up; ready for anything
Mags	Let us never forget this fundamental truth: the state has no source of money other than money which people earn themselves. If the state wishes to spend, it can do so only by borrowing your savings or by taxing you more. It is no good thinking that someone else will pay – that 'someone else' is you. There is no such thing as public money; there is only taxpayers' money
Denis	Well, there's the North Sea oil and gas money And the money from all the public industries you're selling off That's flooding the old coffers isn't it, Boss?
T	Pardon?
Mags	Don't try to pull the wool over my eyes Denis Never Said any of that
Footman	Ladies and gentlemen Pray be upstanding for Her Majesty the Queen

Q and Liz enter through the audience, shaking people's hands. Asking questions such as: 'Did you enjoy the interval?' 'Are you a regular theatregoer?' 'Do you live far away?' 'Very friendly staff here, don't you think?'

Q	That was most enjoyable We met everyone, all the stage management

	They went to such trouble (*To Footman.*) Thank you
Liz	I thought the canapés were rather dry.
Q	Where are we?
T	My second term, Your Majesty
Q	(*wearily*) Oh yes
Mags	We were unleashing new forces in the land
T	Old orders everywhere were being questioned The unions, the NHS, the BBC and yes the Palace
Liz	It felt as if the Palace and I had been shifted – Bottom priority in your Number Ten
Q	We had to provide value for money
Liz	I ask you – the Royal Family
Q	She started cancelling our meetings
T	They were always a distraction
Mags	One was pulled away from whatever one was doing And one was doing an awful lot
Liz	One wouldn't have minded if it was for matters of state
Q	But one week she put us off to entertain some Swedes
	Mags curtsies.
Liz	I thought we might walk out in the grounds today, Prime Minister It's such a pleasant evening and the dogs could come
Mags	Of course, Your Majesty

T	A whole hour wasted in the chill And those dogs . . .
Liz	I was in Kenya when my father died. I remember sitting perfectly calmly feeling the future gaping before me
T	Why's she talking about this?
Liz	The local people were terribly kind. They simply lined the road as we drove back to Nairobi, heads bowed in respect
Mags	The whole Empire grieved for him
Liz	The press were wonderful too Not one camera was raised Not one photograph was taken; not one. Their hats were off, to the last man
Mags	Really?
Liz	Hard to believe now, isn't it?
Q	Michael, would you mind filling the young people in?
Shea	Not at all, Ma'am I'm Michael Shea, the Queen's press secretary I'm a Scot and I'll have a go at the accent. I have a background in diplomacy And I also write thrillers under a pseudonym Pretty good ones in fact –
Q	You can skip that
Shea	The tone of the press had changed towards the Palace. In previous times it had been universally reverential
Murd	The press had basically printed whatever fawning flummery the Palace had given them. But I wasn't going to have that in my papers.

I'm Rupert Murdoch, obviously.
When I bought *The Sun* in 1968 it was a soggy
broadsheet. And I said to the editor – you're
now part of a tabloid revolution. I want a
tearaway paper with lots of tits in it. I bought
The Times and the *Sunday Times* in 1981. I was
doing the same thing there

Liz   Prime Minister, I am worried about the pressure
being put on my children – especially the Prince
and Princess of Wales

Murd   Princess of Sales

Shea   Diana was hounded by the press wherever she
went

Murd   Complained all the time – but she loved it too

Shea   I organised an informal lunch for the editors of
the papers to meet the Queen, so that she might
voice her concerns

Q   It is hard on a girl if she can't even go to the
local sweet shop without being cornered by
photographers

Murd   One of my editors replied: 'Why couldn't she
send a footman for the sweets?'

Q   I think that is the most pompous remark I have
ever heard in my life

Liz   Prime Minister, you have a better relationship
with Mr Murdoch than I

Mags   Your Majesty, freedom of the press is one of the
things upon which true democracy is founded

Liz   I quite agree
But I must lay my family's predicament before
you

Q   This conversation never happened
           We never walked in the garden
           It would have been too hard on Mrs Thatcher's
           heels

Mags   Mr Murdoch may not be a monarchist
           But he's a very good thing for a free press
           The print unions have had their way too long
           And Murdoch will take on the closed shop

Actor 1   What's a closed shop?

Actor 2   The reason actors used to earn proper money
           Bar. After

Murd   If corporations ran things we'd all be better off
           I believe in as little government as possible
           As few rules as possible
           I'm not saying it should be taken to the absolute
           limit
           But I'll spend my whole career pushing it

Mags   We have to trust business and industry to
           regulate itself

Liz   Then may one ask about the economy?
           Because it strikes one that the caps and the
           controls you have removed from our financial
           institutions –

Mags   The greater freedoms we have given

Liz   – are widening the gap

T   What gap?

Liz   Between the rich and poor

Mags   The country is getting richer. For the first time
           we have working-class people buying shares and
           owning homes

Liz	But what about those who are not working? There are more children living in poverty than ever
Mags	How can one relieve their poverty, unless it is by creating wealth? I know that socialists regard the pursuit of wealth as an evil, but right-minded people must surely see it as a good
Liz	But the culture that seems to be prevalent, This insatiable materialism –
T	Has she forgotten she's the world's wealthiest woman?
Liz	One sees these young men in the city really revelling in greed – lording it over the unemployed
T	And there we have it. The true rise of the working class. My barrow boys in the city – that's what she can't brook
Mags	I believe in the working class; not the shirking class
Q	How can she reel off these ludicrous slogans to me?
T	I didn't
Mags	People remain poor because they know they will get state handouts We want to encourage them to get up, to seek work, to make money
Liz	Prime Minister, we've travelled a great deal this year As we do every year And the problem is not just in Britain. The poor are getting poorer

	And we have seen first hand
	The growing gap
T	It would be impolite to mention the fact that Her Majesty, Even as she championed the poor, Paid no tax until 1993 –
Liz	I had some very interesting talks with Mrs Gandhi on my visit to India recently and her view is that the uncontrolled free market is widening the gap –
Mags	With respect, Indira Gandhi was a radical communist in her youth
T	The wealth created by a free economy will trickle down
Liz	Thank you for listening, Prime Minister
Denis	We had some smashing people down at Chequers for Christmas that year. Jeffrey and Mary Archer came We had the Murdochs The Hamiltons; lovely couple The Krays – just joking Dear old Crawfie Carol And after the turkey we turned on the gogglebox for Her Maj
Liz	The greatest problem in the world today remains the gap between rich and poor countries
Mags	What?
Q	My Christmas broadcast Jolly good one that year
Liz	We can ignore the messages we don't like to hear but –

Mags	What's she talking about?
Liz	– we shall not begin to close this poverty gap until we hear less about nationalism and more about interdependence
Mags	That is quite wrong
Liz	One of the main aims of the Commonwealth is to make an effective contribution towards redressing the economic balance between nations
T	Denis
Mags	Denis, she's flouting our policies The entire British effort is to distance ourselves –
Liz	We in the Commonwealth are fortunate enough To belong to a world wide comradeship
Mags, T *and* **Denis**	*Comradeship?*
Liz	Let us make the most of it Only then can we make the message of the angels come true: 'Peace on earth, goodwill towards men'
Mags	Good God
Liz	God bless you all
T	Is Her Majesty a socialist?
Denis	I don't think she's an actual Trot, old love
Mags	Then why, in her Christmas speech, is she expressing dubiously socialistic principles?
Q	They are in fact Christian principles And as Head of the Church One must freely express them
T	We were being undermined

Mags	Your Majesty, I'm sorry to tell you that your Christmas message has been interpreted, by some, as divergent to government policy
Liz	Really?
Mags	It is your government's aim to reduce Commonwealth claims on the British taxpayer. Whatever your personal sentiments are, constitutionally you must ally yourself with your government
Liz	I have a duty to the Commonwealth as well as to my government
T	None of this was said This is all crass surmise
Liz	I vowed that duty before God. It is not something I can bend to / your convenience
Mags	If I may continue
Liz	You are asking me to / tear myself in two
Mags	If I may, your first duty –
Liz	I have pledged a duty / as Head of the Commonwealth
Mags	Your first duty is to the British people Not to a collection of nations Run by communists and mendicants
T	I never said that
Liz	She cut me off She actually cut me off
Q	Attila the hen I think that was Denis Healey
Liz	Who called her The Maggietollah?

Q   One had to laugh

T   The Palace found our fervour for improvement
        funny. It was hurtful

Liz   You held the Commonwealth in contempt
        And that attitude trickled down

Q   The new free market wealth did not

ELEVEN: BOMBS II

Liz   I was in the United States on a private visit to
        inspect some American studs
        When the news came that a bomb had exploded
        at the Conservative Party conference in Brighton

Q   When any great disaster happens where there is
        loss of life
        One feels a physical sense of dread

Liz   It was hard to get accurate news at first
        No one knew how many casualties there were –
        or whom

Mags   It was three a.m. I was putting the finishing
        touches to the next day's speech, when –

        An explosion is heard.

T   The second it happened I thought
        I'm amazed this hasn't happened before

Mags   The noise
        Windows blown to smithereens
        I thought Denis –

T   It was like an earthquake

Denis   Margaret –

Mags	But the lights stayed on
T	In the corridor, people were thrown against walls The bathroom gone in a cloud of dust
Mags	One always imagines that one will be plunged into darkness at a moment like that But the lights stayed on
T	I was still in my evening gown from the night before. Had I been in that bathroom I would not have . . .
Mags	I would have . . .
T	We were very lucky
Denis	Put your speech in the bag If it's in your handbag it won't get lost
Q	There were five dead, Others with terrible injuries Four floors of the hotel had collapsed
T	It was an attempt to destroy, to cripple, to wipe out Her Majesty's democratically elected government. That is the scale of the outrage
Liz	When I was eventually put through Before I could even speak Mrs Thatcher said
Mags	Are you having a wonderful time?
Q	Wasn't that strange? Wasn't that a peculiar response? Such bizarre forced jollity At a moment like that
Liz	Margaret, are you all right?
Mags	Yes, thank you. We are fine

Liz	You must be experiencing very deep shock
Mags	Of course one isn't thinking of oneself One is thinking of the injured And the victims
Liz	Of course Have they given you lots of tea? Tea is terribly good for shock
Q	I didn't know what else to say
Mags	I am perfectly, perfectly fine and untouched
Liz	Philip and I are watching images as they come through on the news It is dreadful
Mags	Thank you so much for your kind concern. There's a Marks and Spencer's
Liz	Pardon?
Mags	We're sending out to Marks and Spencer's We need clothes They're helping us with all the delegates who came out in pyjamas And we're going on –
Liz	Are you?
Mags	– with the conference. We're going on
Q	We watched her speech the next day Not a hair out place
Liz	She made reference to the atrocity and then she just carried on
Mags	The fact that we are gathered here now, shocked but composed and determined, is a sign that not only has this attack failed but that all attempts to destroy democracy through terrorism will fail

Q	Profoundly impressive But at what cost?
Denis	After Brighton, I started thinking she should look to an end You know, towards getting out
Q	Two weeks later, Indira Gandhi was assassinated outside her own home
Liz	Mrs Thatcher brought me the news
Mags	It wasn't terrorists or strangers. It was two of her own personal guards
Liz	Good God
Mags	One of them discharged three rounds into her abdomen. And then his accomplice opened fire on her as she lay on the ground
Q	They removed thirty bullets from her body
Liz	She feared that something like this might happen
Mags	One does fear it, doesn't one
T	No, no, it wasn't fear that I felt; it wasn't fear
Q	It's not fear exactly. One just knows it could be over – that quickly
Liz	If I die a violent death – the violence will be in the thought of my assassin, not in my dying
Mags	Who said that?
Liz	Indira She knew. One cannot make so many enemies And not know
T	It was her own trusted men that did it. That's what I could not brook

Liz	Are you all right?
Mags	After Brighton the IRA said Today we were unlucky But remember, we only have to be lucky once. You will have to be lucky always
Q	Yes; it was chilling
Mags	The hatred in it And the number of people The number of people in this country who Who wish they had got me
Liz	I'm sure that can't be true
Mags	Well, they didn't get me I am not that easy to dispose of And as long as there is breath in my body I will –
Liz	Would you like a scone, Prime Minister?
Mags	Thank you
T	Denis bought me a watch Unusual gesture of affection Engraved on it is 'Every minute counts' I won't waste one of them
Liz	The jam is home-made There's damson and that one's bilberry
Q	I didn't say that We never have bilberry jam
Liz	One likes to support the village fetes around Sandringham One's always buying little jars at local sales of work
Mags	I think one's always looking for the jam that tastes like home. No one made jam like my

mother could. She was very much a woman of the home and I can remember the smell of her gooseberry like it was yesterday

Liz I don't think there's a woman of our whole generation who can't make jam

Q And marmalade

Mags We all learnt from the homily of housekeeping
And I still believe it would save many a financier from failure

Liz You see sometimes it could almost be nice

TWELVE: WET WET WET

T Wets

Mags Do you know what a 'wet' is?

T My backbench was full of them
I knew the enemy across the floor in the House
The Left

T *and* **Mags**
Kinnochio

T I had that enemy in my sights
Where I could squeeze and pulverise it
But another enemy began to appear

Q She changed after Brighton

T *and* **Mags**
Wets

Q One spoke with people in her own party and the feeling was that she was rather cutting herself off

T	These were often the old grandees
	Dripping with titles, land and wealth
	Not like Norman Tebbit and me

Mags   Wets and ultra wets

T   Spineless

Q   One sees it again and again
The longer a leader serves
The less open they become

Mags   Our monarch
I'm sorry to tell you
Is wet

T   We never said that

Liz   For a Methodist, she's remarkably unchristian

Q   We never said that

Liz   One wondered if she was a religious person

Q   No one didn't

Liz   Yes one did
One talked about it with the Archbishop

Q   Oh yes

Liz   He felt sure she had faith but he wasn't sure that
the doctrine of grace meant much to her

Howe   Geoffrey Howe, Foreign Secretary. I wasn't a wet

Mags   Yes you were

Howe   No I wasn't, Margaret. I was one of your own
I sat by your side with Willie Whitelaw
And I must say I heard one question more and
more often

T   Where's Willie?

Howe	No. Is he one of us? Whose side is he on? About people in our own party
Mags	Sometimes I think you're dripping, Geoffrey A big wet sheep
Q	She bullied poor Geoffrey terribly
Howe	I think one of the things that you never fully absorbed, Margaret, is that it's bad management as well as bad manners to reproach as it were officers in front of other ranks

Mags *and* **T**
Oh dear

Howe	If you want to tick people off or have arguments with them then you should, as a matter of courtesy, do it in private
Mags	You are Foreign Secretary. Foreign affairs are interesting, Geoffrey – they are interesting! And your endless drone has the whole Cabinet comatose
Howe	You are becoming increasingly reckless, if you like, of the way in which you conduct your personal relationships
Mags	Go and tell Crawfie I'm ready for my comb-out
T	To be wet is to be like a soggy August The whole concept reminded me of Balmoral
Q	I'm sorry to tell you that Mrs Thatcher didn't care for Balmoral
T	Bagpipes Wellingtons Torment

Q	She came for three days every year like all my PM's
Liz	Harold Wilson brought his dogs We always had a jolly time
Mags	I said, Crawfie, pack something warm For heaven's sake pack thermals
Liz	We love throwing on a head scarf and striding over the moors And we especially love our picnics
T	It's an unnerving experience Prince Philip cooking drumsticks under damp tarpaulins Eating with Tupperware on the side of a wind-blown hill
Liz	Would you like the gherkins, Mrs Thatcher?
Mags	I'll get them Let me serve them Let me pass them round Your Royal Highness, would you like a gherkin?
Liz	She kept on jumping up to help But we enjoy serving people at our picnics
Mags	It completely dismayed me
T	The Queen, rolling up her sleeves to rinse the mugs
Mags	Let me do that Your Majesty, I'm a dab hand with the washing up – Let me
Q	Philip said
Philip	Someone tell that bloody woman to sit down
T	It was more stressful than a NATO summit

Q	I know our life up there does not appeal to everyone But it is home And when one opens it to guests –
Liz	She used to leave at six in the morning Really as soon as she could One found it rude
Shea	Michael Shea again Mrs Thatcher's style became ever more regal She began to use the royal 'we'
Mags	I am not an 'I did this' 'I did that' person. I have never been an 'I' person. I prefer to talk about 'we' – the government . . . It is not I who do things, it is we, the government
T	We have become a grandmother
Q	Have you come to talk about 1986?
Shea	Yes I have
Q	I expect a lot of you were not yet born Or still at school Or listening to all those dreadful bands Diana used to like
Shea	In 1986
T	Prince Andrew got married to Sarah Ferguson. A lovely wedding
Shea	I wasn't going to talk about that
Liz	The press called her an unbrushed red setter trying to get out of a potato sack. I thought that was a bridge too far
T	The Queen's trooping horse Burmese retired after seventeen years
Shea	I wasn't going to talk about that either

T   Well, what else are you qualified to talk about?

Shea   I was going to talk about your decision to allow
        America to bomb Libya, using Britain as its base

T   The Queen has no wish to discuss that

Q   Yes I do
        She let Reagan send his planes from our air bases
        None of the other NATO countries would

Liz   And I was the last to know

Actor 2 There was an all-time hullaballoo in the House.
        I would like to remind the Right Honourable
        Lady –

Actor 1 Who are you being?

Actor 2 Kinnock

Actor 1 I'm Kinnock

Actor 2 You're Michael Shea

Actor 1 I can be Kinnock and Shea

Actor 2 Then don't miss your chance

Actor 1 (*as Kinnock*) I would like to remind the Right
        Honourable Lady that the hullaballoo came not
        just from the Labour Party but from her own
        back benches, from her own cabinet

T   You're not Kinnock

Kinnock Would the Right Honourable Lady agree that
        there is only one reason why President Reagan
        sought her co-operation?

T   You're not anybody

Kinnock The President knew that when he said jump, she
        would reply, 'How high?'

Q	(*to Actor 1*) Would you be Michael Shea again, please? I think you were about to mention South Africa
Shea	I was about to mention South Africa
Q	Thank you
Shea	The international community was putting pressure on Great Britain to impose sanctions on the apartheid regime
Mags	Britain will not be imposing sanctions on South Africa
Liz	But the Commonwealth has made a pledge to eradicate apartheid
Mags	Ma'am, the ANC is a Marxist Leninist organisation –
Liz	Apartheid, Prime Minister Now we fought against the Nazis And I can see no difference
Mags	Were the ANC to take power, South Africa would be plunged into socialist chaos / and the economy –
Liz	The Commonwealth's position is clear Apartheid is out
Mags	Firstly, anyone who thinks the ANC can form a government is living in cloud cuckoo land –
Liz	/ That's up to the people. Don't forget what you learnt in Zimbabwe
Mags	Secondly, to impose sanctions Would not only plunge the poor into further poverty It would be inimical to British trade

Ron	And American trade
	Margaret and I, yet again we shared a vision . . .
	You know, I attempted to veto US sanctions
	But can you believe it?
	I was overridden by Congress
T	I had Ron's personal support if not his government's
Ron	It was the first time this century that any president was overruled on foreign policy
T	Why did they not see that we were right?
Ron	Margaret, we were just too far ahead sometimes
T	Oh, Ron
Q	She wouldn't listen. She stuck with her opinion
Liz	Alone in the UN, alone in the Commonwealth, in the Commons
Q	Alone in her own Cabinet
Howe	Geoffrey Howe again. The resignations had begun. Michael Heseltine went
T	Jolly good riddance I say
Howe	I think, Margaret, that he felt his views weren't being listened to. I wish I had some Heseltine lines to convey his indignation but I haven't
T	He threw quite a tantrum – stormed out of Cabinet with a flick of his hair
Howe	Then Leon Brittan went. And when Willie Whitelaw retired Margaret lost her best restraining influence
T	Every Prime Minister needs a Willie
Howe	She became more and more reliant on her unelected advisers –

Mags	You are interrupting a scene. The Queen is about to speak
Howe	Beg pardon, Your Majesty
Mags	You haven't even got the correct year. Willie retired in '87 and we are still in '86
Howe	Oh
Mags	Why don't you go away until you have your facts right?
Liz	One sees black South Africans seeking basic human rights Being violently oppressed – Surely this is this very thing That you abhor in communist countries? The utter lack of freedom And the brutal state control?
Mags	The political science here Is quite different
Q	So patronising
Liz	There comes a time When morally One must say no
Mags	I welcome your point of view I value your advice. Thank you for the tea-cake, Your Majesty

THIRTEEN: BREAKFAST AT HOLYROOD

Q	One suspects she is racist
T	I am not a racist I am *not* What I feel about the black South Africans

	Is exactly the same as I feel about the Germans
	The Italians, the Greeks
	Or anyone else not blessed to be British

Mags   I never said that

Q   But your attitude trickled down

Shea   Michael Shea again
The Commonwealth Games were held in
Edinburgh that year
The opening ceremony was spectacular
Five thousand children in a human mosaic

Liz   But Michael, thirty-two nations have boycotted
in protest
Hardly an African country there – because of
her intransigence on sanctions

Shea   The Games were indeed looking very white

Liz   It cannot be borne. It simply cannot

Shea   Something had to be done
Of course I didn't do it
I didn't do anything at all

Mags and Liz open newspapers.

On July the twentieth, the *Sunday Times*
Announced Her Majesty's dismay
At the policies of the government

T   It was a huge, huge spread

Q *and* **T**   Pages

Shea   The journalists
Michael Jones, political editor
And Simon Freeman (backstabbing bastard)
Claimed irrefutable evidence
That the Queen found her Prime Minister

T	Uncaring, confrontational and socially divisive
Shea	It was very precise
T	The journalists said the Queen was fully aware it would be published
Shea	Here are the bullet points. One:
Liz	One feared that the suppression of the miners' strike had done long-term damage to the fabric of the state
Shea	Two:
Liz	One objected to America's bombing raids on Libya departing from British airbases
Shea	Three:
Liz	One supported sanctions in South Africa and abhorred apartheid
Shea	Four:
Liz	One had deep concerns about our own disintegrating race relations and inner-city decay
Shea	And that overall
Liz	One felt the whole direction of government policy was –
T	What a betrayal
Q	Never said it Never wrote it Nothing to do with me
T	For an unelected monarch To oppose the government – Unconstitutional and dangerous
Shea	Ironically we were together when the news broke One of the rare occasions I was with them both

The Queen
The Prime Minister and myself
At Holyrood in Edinburgh
It was breakfast time

Mags and Liz are both reading the revelations.

Shea   Well, I couldn't eat a thing
The silence was so sickening

T   I didn't trust myself to speak
I wasn't angry; it's not that.
I was surprised

Q   It was her friend Mr Murdoch's paper
I felt like leaping up and saying there
There you are
This is what it's like when the papers turn on you
No one is safe from a ruthless press

Shea   The Prime Minister's face was quite unmoving

Liz   Well
One wonders how this happened, Michael

Shea   I'd like to apologise
Profusely to you both
Your Majesty
Prime Minister
Yes, it's true I did meet Simon Freeman
And we were talking off the record
Quite informally
And he asked about the Commonwealth
I replied that as Head of the Commonwealth
The Queen . . .
Is naturally very keen on it
And so forth
The rest is all his supposition
Prime Minister, I can assure you that

I had no briefing with Her Majesty

The Queen had no prior knowledge of this article
And indeed
I have never, ever heard her
Speaking critically of you
Or any of her previous Prime Ministers

Shea Mrs Thatcher said only three words to me:

Mags Never mind, dear

Shea That was it

T Never mind, dear

Shea It was the most excruciating breakfast I was ever at

Pause.

T I was knocked sideways
I was very, very down

Liz Margaret
I'm sorry this has happened

Mags Thank you, Ma'am
Really I am so respectful

Liz That is mutual, you know

FOURTEEN: THE WORLD WON'T LISTEN

Q The President of the United States
May only serve for two terms

Liz No matter how powerful one's allies are, they are passing.
There is no permanence in politics

Q I've spent a lifetime in the ebb and flow of power
It brings its gifts

	But then it's an intoxicant One must beware lest one consumes too much
T	We tried to advise and assist George Bush as we had Ron, but he didn't seem so –
Mags	He didn't have Ron's friendly personality And sadly we disagreed over Germany
T	No one but me could see the threat of reunification
Mags	We've beaten the Germans twice and we don't want them back
Howe	Her attitude to Europe confounded me
T	Are you back, Geoffrey? You'd better have something worthwhile to say
Mags	We have not rolled back the frontiers of the state in Britain only to see them reimposed at a European level
Howe	She could undo the careful work of a whole conference with a single utterance
Mags	No No NO
Clarke	Kenneth Clarke, Education Secretary Margaret began to believe her own propaganda; she began to fly by the seat of her pants. She began to get more scratchy. And the poll tax – what a disaster. Geoffrey, explain what it was, would you? I have to be Kinnock
Howe	Margaret felt the rating system put too much pressure on home-owners, so the poll tax, or community charge –
T	If Geoffrey explains we'll still be here at breakfast time tomorrow

Kinnock The community charge is the most flagrantly unjust taxation we have seen since the Peasants' Revolt in 1381

T The community charge is the flagship of the Thatcher fleet.
I can defend it clearly, explicitly, at any time, in any place and to any person

Liz So how does it work then?

Mags It is designed to prevent overspending left-wing councils from squeezing home-owners any further. Everyone pays the same

Liz A bus driver in his council flat pays the same as the Duke of Westminster in his mansion – have I got that correct?

Mags Yes. And you, Ma'am, pay nothing at all

Kinnock It is fundamentally unfair, costly and crushing to families

Howe Margaret thought her will alone could push it through – but she got the mood of the people wrong

Q The people didn't think her tax was fair
They refused to pay it – and they rioted

Protestor No, they demonstrated

Mags They were anarchists and scum

Protestor Two hundred thousand citizens marched peacefully up Whitehall

Mags The rabble set Trafalgar Square on fire. The looting and rampaging, violence and destruction went on for hours

T I was brought up to respect law and order

Protestor The police blocked both ends of Whitehall, so the crowd couldn't disperse. Then, with no warning, they sent in the riot squad

Mags We are moving on

Protestor No we're not.
I am protesting.
By three o'clock, the police had corralled us into Trafalgar Square. How to turn citizens into a mob? Charge at them on horses. Drive through them in riot vans at high speed. Fear makes you defend yourself; it is incendiary. Demonstrators became rioters and on that day the act of protest was made criminal

Howe I feared her flagship was sinking

T I was brought up by a Victorian grandmother

Mags You were taught to respect law and order, to work jolly hard, to improve yourself, you were taught self-reliance, you lived within your income

T You were patriotic, you had self-respect, you were a good member of your community

Mags These things are Victorian Values

Howe She was losing her touch. Opinion polls were very low. By-elections disastrous

T In the Cabinet I could almost hear knives being sharpened

Q It's rare for a leader to know when to go

Mags I will go on to win a fourth term and a fifth – as long as the people want me and Britain needs me

Howe	I knew when to go
	This is my resignation speech

Q   Not all of it Geoffrey, please

Howe I'll cut the references to cricket, Ma'am
      The conflict of loyalty, of loyalty to my Right
      Honourable Friend the Prime Minister and of
      loyalty to what I perceive to be the true interests
      of the nation, has become all too great

Mags His was a slow poison

Howe I no longer believe it possible to resolve that
      conflict from within this Government. That is
      why I have resigned

Mags That quiet voice of his

Howe The time has come for others to consider their
      own response to the tragic conflict of loyalties
      with which I have myself wrestled for perhaps
      too long

T   He gave them permission to revolt

Liz   Philip showed me a cartoon from *The Times* the
      next day. It was of Geoffrey Howe as a huge
      sheep, swallowing Mrs Thatcher whole – just
      her heels sticking out. A caption read 'Howe's
      That?'

Mags I will call their bluff

T   Flush the traitors out

Mags If they want a leadership challenge
      By golly I'll give them one

T   I'm a world stateswoman

Mags On the verge of committing our troops to Kuwait

T   I'm a proven election-winner

Mags	And I can count on my party to back me to the hilt
T	When someone says you have a contest, you do not run away, you fight it
Mags	Come on, boys Let's have a leadership challenge Who's up to it? Who thinks that they can take me on?
Hesel	I've been waiting years for this
T	The mighty Heseltine
Hesel	I've sat long enough on the back benches
Mags	Festering
Hesel	Watching as you've estranged the brightest and the best in your Cabinet. You never appreciated my contribution and you took credit for all my triumphs
T	It's all about you isn't it, Michael?
Hesel	This party would have got on just as well and achieved just as much without you, Margaret
Mags	That is preposterous
Hesel	When I was at Oxford, I plotted my future on an envelope
Mags	I bet you did
Hesel	Millionaire twenty-five – and I was MP thirty – and I was Cabinet member – yes
Mags	And Prime Minister? I don't think so, Hezza
Hesel	They say a man should be judged by his enemies. I am very proud of mine

T	Tarzan stood against me
Hesel	I am the man to lead Britain into the 1990s

FIFTEEN: DIAMONDS ARE FOREVER

Mags	I was in Paris for the first vote Bush, Mitterrand, Gorbachev, Kohl They were all there
T	I was advised to stay at home and canvass people in the Commons tea room. I ask you. I was Prime Minister
Mags	The vote was counted as I was signing one of the treaties that ended the Cold War. Denis phoned me through the news
Denis	You did very well, old love. But not well enough. You're four votes short. I'm afraid there's got to be a second round
T	Ever so slightly, the ground shifted under my feet
Denis	It's the rules, sweetie pie
Mags	I'm going forward, Denis The party will rally now In my hour of need they'll come back to me
Denis	I knew then she was done for
T	That night, Crawfie and I stayed up. We talked
Mags	Grantham
T	School
Mags	The horrible headmistress who attempted to thwart my ambition
T	Oxford

Mags	How they tried to look down on me
T	Denis
Mags	My twins
T	The way I would often forget to wave up at the nursery window on my way to work
Mags	As dawn came we were still talking. We didn't go to bed at all
Liz	At our audience on her return, the Prime Minister told me she'd contest the second ballot –
Mags	I shall carry on batting for Britain, with all the vigour and energy I have
Q	What could one say?
Liz	As a human being, one always has hope – and the gambling instinct
Q	We did not put money on it
Clarke	Kenneth Clarke. Margaret said she wanted to see us, one by one. I was first in
Mags	Kenneth, can I count on your support?
Clarke	Look, Margaret, this whole process is farcical. It's time to go. Do you really want to see Michael Heseltine Prime Minister? It's time to clear the field for Douglas Hurd or Major; someone who can win
T	At least Kenneth Clarke stabbed me in the front
Mags	A dismal procession followed
T	Old school ties and sweating brows. One of them even cried

Tory 2   I will vote for you, Margaret

Tory 1   I am on your side

Tory 2   You know you have my loyalty

Tory 1   I'd walk on broken glass for you

Tory 2   Stick hot pins

Tory 1   But honestly?

Tory 2   I don't think any of the others

Tory 1   Nobody will vote your way

Tory 2   The support just isn't there

T   The message was clear

Tory 1 *and* **2**
             You will never win

Mags   I considered you my friends and allies and it
             disgusts me that with your weasel words you
             have transmuted your betrayal into frank
             advice. It sickens me that you pretend concern
             for my fate. Because this is treachery. It is
             treachery with a smile on its face
             I've have won three elections and I could go on
             without you. By God I have deserved it. I've
             done everything for years. Not one of you could
             have achieved one-tenth

Denis   Margaret
             Give it up
             Give it up, old girl
             Come on

Mags   I am not a quitter
             I am not a quitter

Denis   Let it go

93

Pause.

T	And so The following morning I went once more to my Cabinet
Mags	And I stood down As their leader As Prime Minister
T	I then telephoned world leaders
Mags	There was utter disbelief
T	Bush said some very gracious things And then he asked about my successor
Mags	I was already history I was exhausted. Found it very difficult to –
T	Crawfie called a doctor. Got a vitamin shot And when I was back on my feet again, I went to the Palace
Q	Mrs Thatcher sat where she had sat every week for the last eleven years. She told me she was going to stand down
Liz	That must have been a very difficult decision
Mags	You don't take a decision like that without it being difficult Without there being heartbreak Yes, there is heartbreak But it is the right thing
Liz	Mrs Thatcher's emotion was not perceptible in anything she said. Her effort to contain it was remarkable
Q	It was the same for me when our Royal Yacht Britannia was decommissioned. I was resolutely determined that no tears would be seen to fall

Liz	The last few days must have been traumatic for you
Mags	Yes But we got through them And tonight we will leave Number Ten for the –
T	For the last time
Liz	Would you like a whisky?
Mags	Thank you, Ma'am
Liz	I shall have my Gin and It One tries to keep everything together One does one's very best But sometimes the harder one holds on, the more things fall apart. I fear there are some tricky times ahead
Mags	For you, Ma'am?
Liz	My children are all unhappy If they had privacy they might have found a private solace but There is a crisis brewing, Margaret. Charles and Diana cannot reconcile And I won't have divorce I will not, cannot have it
Liz	Here's to certainty
All	To certainty
	They drink.
Mags	I hope that in my years at Number Ten I have done what I set out to do
Liz	You have achieved a great deal; that, no one can deny
Mags	I set out to change the soul of this country

Q	How very disturbing
Liz	And now, where will you go?
Mags	To the back benches I won't shirk it I'll confound them all
Q	You always have
Liz	Where will you live?
Mags	We've a house in Dulwich Denis chose it Spanking new Right next to his golf course On the South Circular
Liz	I'm sure it will be an exciting new chapter
Mags	It will never happen to you, Your Majesty
Liz	I'm sorry?
Mags	You will never relinquish your power
Liz	But Prime Minister In our democracy I have none
Q	How do you do? How do you do?
T	We regard the Royal Family as the greatest asset Britain has. They are a focus of patriotism, loyalty, affection and esteem.
Liz	When one sees you in the House And hears them baying at you One can't imagine how you keep your poise They really are so dreadful Like an awful pack of schoolboys
Mags	Yes, they can be odious

But I thrive on it, you see
I stand out in my blue and blond
And I thrive

Liz Quite so

Mags Without it I'm not sure what I will do

Q That afternoon, she took Prime Minister's
Questions in the House. We watched her on the
television

Liz Her performance was pure Iron Lady

Mags The Berlin Wall has been torn down and the
Cold War is at an end. These immense changes
didn't come about by chance. They have been
achieved by resolution in defence – and by a
refusal ever to be intimidated. And all these
things were done in teeth of the opposition of
the Right Honourable Gentlemen opposite –
and their ladies
Should we be censured for our strength?
It is because we on this side have never flinched
from difficult decisions
That this House
And this country
Can have confidence in this government today

Mags exits.

Footman 1
The atmosphere on the street is amazing,
Ma'am. There are people dancing out there,
shouting 'She's gone, she's gone'

Liz Really

Footman 2
Absolute jubilation

Actor 1	Do you remember it?
Actor 2	It was amazing. A tremendous feeling that anything could happen That . . .
Actor 1	That what?
Actor 2	That things could only get better

Actors 1 and 2 exit.

Liz	It is affecting when they go One doesn't have time to turn around Out goes the last and in comes the next with barely a pause And one has often built up a relationship

Liz exits.

Q	Of course stories about clashes
T	Nonsense
Q	There was never any question
T	Stories about clashes
Q	There was never a rift
T	We have always loved the Queen
Q	The Baroness read out the eulogy when Ronald Regan died It was impeccable
T	We here still move in twilight But we have a beacon to guide us We have his example Let us give thanks for a life that achieved so much for all of God's children
Q	I would have put it slightly differently The fortieth President

Like Michael Shea our dear Press Secretary
Died of dementia

T   One doesn't die of dementia, Ma'am,
      It is not a fatal condition
      One dies of something else.
      One lives with dementia

      They are both standing.

Q   Won't you sit down?

      Pause.

T   No.

      The End.